LAND YOUR DREAM JOB

JOIN THE 2% WHO MAKE IT PAST RESUMÉ SCREENING

MICHAEL LACHANCE

I would like to dedicate this book to the following people:

Family and Friends

Through thick and thin, I could not have asked for a better group of people to navigate life's waters with. Thank you for always supporting and encouraging me.

Self-Publishing School

So much in my personal and professional life has improved since joining this incredible company. As they say, "find a job you love, and you'll never work a day in your life." Self-Publishing School has provided me with a job I love and much, much more.

YOU!

Now that I've landed my dream job, I'd encourage YOU to do the same.

Discover the EXACT three-step blueprint you need to become a bestselling author in three months.

Self-Publishing School helped me, and now I want them to help you with this FREE WEBINAR!

Even if you're busy, bad at writing, or don't know where to start, you CAN write a bestseller and build your best life.

With tools and experience across a variety of niches and professions, Self-Publishing School is the only resource you need to take your book to the finish line!

Don't Wait

Watch this FREE WEBINAR now, and Say "YES" to becoming a bestseller:

[https://xe172.isrefer.com/go/sps4fta-vts/bookbrosinc6600]

Important Note

In some chapters of this book, the cover letter and resumé formatting is incorrect. Due to the size of the book, it's not possible to accurately portray my cover letter and resumé samples on a single page. Please see the "Sample" chapters for an accurate representation of how your cover letter and resumé should be formatted or go to

fb.me/LandYourDreamJob

for more details.

Thanks for understanding!

PAUL WANTED to land his dream job. Problem was, he applied to lots of jobs but never secured an interview. In fact, he didn't hear back from most companies he applied to. After a few months of frustration, no income, and no career development, he finally came to visit me in the Career Resource Centre.

Frustrated and desperate, Paul exclaimed, "I've applied to ten jobs in the past week alone. I haven't heard back from a single one. How am I going to afford rent? Or move out of my parents' house? I need a job yesterday!"

"I have good news," I responded. "You have so much potential to improve your job application."

I looked down at his resumé again. "The first thing I'd suggest is reorganizing the structure of your resumé. It's difficult to read, and hiring managers do not have time to go through your experience with a fine-toothed comb. Second, I notice you're not communicating the value you'll bring to the company. The hiring manager won't hire you if they don't think you're a valuable candidate. Let's look at the job description for the position you're applying for."

"I didn't bring the job description. I've already listed my past employment experience on my resumé. I even listed the duties I was responsible for, see?" said Paul, pointing to a few bulleted words on his resumé.

"That's not good enough for a hiring manager," I said bluntly. "Listing duties is not proving to the hiring manager you're a strong candidate for this position. First, you need to understand exactly what the hiring manager needs. That's why we need the job description. Second, you need to communicate how your experience will provide value to those needs."

Paul realized that he should have asked for help with his job application months ago. Our short conversation made him realize that he was not thinking like a hiring manager.

Two weeks after Paul improved his cover letter and resumé, he came back to visit me all smiles. I helped him land his dream job.

This made me wonder how many candidates out there, like Paul, were still struggling to secure their dream jobs. I looked into some statistics and came across this quote from Robert Meier, president of Job Market Experts:

"98% of job seekers are eliminated at the initial resumé screening" and only the "Top 2% of candidates make it to the interview."

Paul was part of the 98% before he came to see me in the Career Resource Centre. Like you, his goal was to join the two percent that makes it past resumé screening.

But where did you and the rest of the 98% of candidates go wrong?

To put it simply, you're not giving the employer what they need. You're not positioning your cover letter and resumé to hit the bullseye of employer's needs. Or, you're making a few minor mistakes which disqualify you from the hiring process.

Maybe it's because you don't know how to present your work experience. Or you have heard so many strategies you just don't know what to do anymore.

Whatever it is, no job means no paycheck, no career development, no chance of moving up the corporate ladder.

After being rejected from the hiring process this many times, you're getting desperate.

Maybe you've tried the shotgun approach, sending your resumé to every job opening in your town. You sent out so many applications, one has to land you a job, right?

I'm sure you've applied to the same job twice. Doesn't this company know how serious you are about working for them? How many more times do you need to apply before they notice your resumé? Why haven't they called you for an interview yet?

Limited help is available. We all know our high school's Career Studies course didn't teach us much. My teacher was more than socially awkward. How was he going to teach me how to communicate my skills to an employer effectively?

That's where I come in.

In this book, you will learn how to transition from rejected to hired. You will develop from a reactive candidate (one who waits to hear from an employer) to a proactive candidate with a plan of attack to get hired.

You'll learn how to look at a job description and know exactly what the employers are looking for in their ideal candidates. This book will also show you how to use this information to create a focused cover letter and resumé for the job you want. You'll also learn strategies to set yourself up for success in your interview.

Most of my experience comes from my Career Services background at Brock University.

As a career assistant at Brock, I supported students, alumni, and faculty with cover letters, resumés, and job search strategies. I helped these folks land their dream job by matching their skills, experience, and degree with their ideal job. I've been trained in interview strategies and have extensive experience interviewing other career assistants.

In this position alone, I reviewed and improved hundreds upon hundreds of resumés and cover letters.

A few years later, I started another job in automotive manufacturing. After being promoted to Quality Control Lab Supervisor, I interviewed candidates seeking to work as lab technicians. I helped develop the job description, conducted interviews, and assisted with hiring decisions.

During this time, I saw the entire hiring process from the perspective of both the candidate and the employer.

In my role as Student Success Representative at Self-Publishing School, one of my responsibilities was screening candidates for a student success coach position.

Over a few short weeks, I developed candidate screening

tests and screened over 500 applications. By the time I finished, I provided a list of 10 A-level candidates to my manager. After reviewing this many applications, you can quickly spot those candidates who have a chance (and those who don't).

For the last 10 years, I've played a major role in changing people's employment lives. But the insight from this book is not only from a hiring manager's perspective. These strategies have worked for my personal (and extensive!) employment history, too.

I've successfully applied to and been hired by over 20 different organizations before turning 30. With five promotions in three very different industries.

I've left every single one of those jobs with good references (well, minus the one job that let me go for being involved in a food fight. Word to the wise: don't start a food fight at a coffee shop while you're the supervisor on shift. You'll probably get fired).

Trust me. I understand what the employer needs from you so you can get this job. I've supported so many candidates, just like you, who were close to giving up on their job search.

When candidates first came into the Career Resource Centre, his or her resumé resembled an unfinished room in a house. It lacked context and value.

Like the unfinished room, their resumé needed purpose to bring it to fruition. If a room lacks purpose, it's because someone didn't understand what it is supposed to be, do, or look like. It's just there, like a rejected candidate's resumé.

But the student left with an achievement-focused resumé that targeted specific skills from the job description—laser focused, like a fighter pilot zeroing in on an enemy plane.

Knowing their resumé was full of context, value, and purpose, the candidate left feeling confident they'd get the next job they applied for.

It was an incredible feeling, having students come back and thank me personally for helping them secure a job. A student once bought me a coffee when she saw me working again after she got hired. She remembered me by name and expressed gratitude for the help I gave her.

This made me feel I made a huge difference in her life.

"Moving up the corporate ladder" starts with that first job, getting your foot on that first rung—and I helped her achieve that. Who knows what kind of success she is having now.

Gone are the days of the shotgun approach to landing your next job. By reading this book, you'll learn to market your experience to provide value and context to your future employer. You'll learn how to communicate your work experience in a way the hiring manager will understand. You will gain confidence you never had before, knowing you are providing employers what they are looking for.

This book is a key that will open many doors of opportunity. But you must know that doors of employment continually close. Every day you wait to use this key is a day lost, and a day of opportunity you've given to another candidate.

Job openings do not last forever. In fact, employers want to fill any job openings as quickly as possible. When you choose to wait, you are choosing to let the opportunity to pass you by.

Don't be the person to lose out on another job opportunity. The fact that 98% of people don't make it past the first resumé screening is not a chance; it is a choice. These candidates did not take action on the information that is now available to them.

The tips you will learn in the next few chapters will dramatically change your understanding of how to write an effective cover letter and resumé. These tips helped me land over 20 jobs.

When I'm looking to hire a new candidate, I'm looking for candidates who apply the tips I clearly lay out in this book.

When comparing the resumés between someone who has received help and someone who hasn't, it's easy for me to decide who'll be invited to the interview.

Let's make sure you're the one who gets the interview.

WHAT IS A COVER LETTER?_

LANDING your dream job starts with building a strong cover letter. In this chapter, I will explain what a cover letter is, and break it down into sections so you can create one yourself. I'll also discuss the purpose of having a cover letter so you can use it effectively.

Before we move further, it's important you understand that the goal of this book is to teach you how to position yourself in the entire job search process.

I don't want you to use a copy of my own because that won't teach you how to create a new and effective cover letter for every job you apply to.

My goal is to provide you with context behind the samples in this book. This way, you'll learn how to apply these skills to different positions as you grow in your professional career. You'll not only learn *what* is important in a cover letter (and resumé) but also *why* it is important.

A cover letter is a one-page document used to entice an

employer to hire you. It consists of three main sections, written in paragraphs.

The first section is the introductory paragraph. Here, you will introduce yourself and blatantly state the job you are applying for.

The middle section will plainly explain how your skills match the company's needs. This is where you want to sell yourself as much as possible to your future employer. This will be the largest paragraph of your cover letter.

The third section is where you include your contact information. You want to make it easy for the employer to contact you for an interview.

The theme of your cover letter is that you are the only candidate worthy of being hired for the position. If you settle for anything less, you're leaving the door of opportunity open for other candidates. Illuminate your passion and desire for the position while highlighting your most relevant qualifications for the job.

You may wish to ponder the following questions as you create your cover letter: what skills, value, and experience are you bringing to the company's table? In what ways will you contribute to this position, the company's short-term and long-term goals?

Fail to explain how you'll bring value to the company and you can kiss your opportunity for a job goodbye.

In the next few pages, I will walk you through each paragraph and make sure you know what to put in each one. But first, I want to share a few important notes with you.

Research the company before you start your cover letter.

Know the company's address and phone number. Know the name of the individual who will receive your cover letter (most likely the hiring manager). If you do not have this information yet, stop reading this book and go look it up. You will need this information before moving forward.

Understanding the position requirements will play a pivotal role in building a strong cover letter. If you don't understand the core skills of the position for which you are applying, you will not show the employer you have the required skills for the position.

Your cover letter may be the only content a prospective employer will ever read about you. This means it is important for you to make every sentence in your cover letter count towards marketing you and your skills. You need to hook your future boss's attention by showing how your experiences will bring value to the company.

One of the most common mistakes I see when reviewing cover letters is that candidates do not match their experience with the required skills of the job. There is a misalignment.

For example, a company may seek strong leadership skills, but the candidate focused their resumé on their varsity and sports experience. That experience is great and all, but the company needs to know you can fill a need in its business.

In this scenario, leadership skills are the need. If you do not make your leadership experience clear, then there is no way the company will hire you for the job!

From this moment forward, your number one goal is to explain what you can do for the employer. NOT what the employer can do for you.

11

As stated above, the hiring manager is looking for candidates to fill a specific need. There is a missing puzzle piece in their organization, and it is your job to articulate why and how you are that missing puzzle piece they require.

As soon as you mention what the company can do for you (for example, saying that getting his job will help advance your career), you are starting the relationship off on the wrong foot. The company is the Alpha in the hiring process—they dictate terms, and your job is to give them what they ask for.

Finding and recruiting new employees can be an exhausting and time-consuming process. Nowadays, some companies use software to filter through job applications to make the process of searching for and hiring new talent easier. Software will scan through job applications to search for specific keywords required for the job.

If companies can automatically exclude all candidates that don't have the experience and skills they are looking for, it's easier for them to focus on the right candidates—those applicants who meet their specific needs.

The problem is, many people don't include skill keywords in their cover letters and resumés. If an employer is looking for people with specific skills—such as team player—but you are not including these words in your cover letter, it is unlikely anyone will view your application. From the software's perspective, you do not have the relevant experience and are therefore not a good candidate.

This software will scan for other factors too. Most job descriptions include a job number, and if you did not include the job number in your cover letter, you probably won't get an invite to the interview.

But have no fear! I will make sure you make none of these costly mistakes.

Now that you know what a cover letter is, and how to use it to land a job, let's focus on building your cover letter the smart way. Let's build a cover letter that will show a future employer how you can—and will—contribute to the company's goals.

In the next chapter, I will show you why it is so important for you to have a cover letter, no matter what job you are applying to.

WHO NEEDS A COVER LETTER?_

IF YOU'RE THINKING of applying to a job without a cover letter (even when it's not requested!), you must understand that you're leaving a huge opportunity on the table.

You're missing out on the opportunity to land your dream job.

A cover letter will explain how your experience will allow you to excel with the company. You can build a relationship with your future employer, explaining how you plan to contribute to their company. Employers won't have to guess or think for themselves on how you'll provide value. It'll paint a picture of your work ethic and personalize your work experience.

Therefore, include a cover letter in your next job application. If you are truly interested in being hired for this job, or if you're tired of waiting for a call to an interview, start your cover letter now.

If you don't include a cover letter in your next application, I can promise you someone else in the applicant pool will. This will put their work experience into context in ways that your stand-alone resumé never will. In truth, you're making it easier for the next candidate to get this job.

Create a brand-new cover letter for every job to which you apply. It does not matter if you're applying to a new job, for a promotion, or even to an old boss—the rule is the same. You need a customized cover letter for each application.

In the introduction to this book, I mentioned that I have held over 20 different employment positions. Every position I applied to had specific needs, and I had to adapt my cover letter for each one to give me the best chance at being hired.

If I used the same cover letter for all 20 jobs, I would not have been maximizing my potential in explaining why I would be a good fit for each company. Some of these positions required more of one skill than another or required certifications that others didn't. I knew the best way to land each job would be to make an individual cover letter for each application focusing on the specific skills required in each position.

———

I can't stress enough how important it is to create a new cover letter for every job application. When I worked at Brock University, I applied for a supervisor position in the Career Resource Centre. In the new position, I would answer to the same boss, sit in the same seat in the same room. Nothing in my work environment would change. Even so, I had to prove to my manager I had the skills and experience it would take to be a supervisor in this new position.

I created a new cover letter when I applied for a promotion

when I worked at Waterville TG Inc., too. I would work for for the same boss. Yet, I wrote a new cover letter to demonstrate that I had the skills and work ethic to deserve the promotion. I didn't want anyone else to get that job due to my lack of action. I had to prove I had the skills my manager needed in this new role.

Creating a new cover letter for every job I applied to—even when applying to the same company—allowed me to put my value into context. I got a promotion in both cases.

———

This brings forth the most important lesson when creating a cover letter. Always focus on how your skills will bring value to the employer. What exactly does the company need that you have experience doing? Make this easy for the company to understand in your cover letter.

You can also minimize concerns an employer may have after they read your resumé. For example, you can explain any gaps in employment history if you haven't been working for a while. Without a cover letter, the company may think you've been lazy or not looking for a job when you had a legitimate reason for not working.

Now that you know you need a cover letter for every job you are applying to, it is time for us to understand the job description to maximize your potential for being hired.

Let's take a look in the next chapter.

THE JOB DESCRIPTION_

Now you know you need a cover letter for every job you apply to. But if you need to make a new cover letter for every job, how are you going to make each one different?

You will use the skills from the job description, of course!

When a company is looking to hire a candidate, they will post a job description for the position. The job description will clearly state the required skills, duties, and attributes of the job. You'll be able to see hours of work, wage information, job location, and any other special demands of the job. All information needed to apply for the position will be in the job description.

A strong cover letter will relate to the job posting directly.

If a company is looking for skills X, Y, and Z, a strong cover letter will show your work experience with skills X, Y, and Z.

Understanding the job description will help you focus your cover letter on the skills that provide the most value for the company. You can research the company beyond the job description to understand what these skills and attributes are.

I suggest you Google as much information about the employer as possible. Where is the company located? How many people work there? What is the company's mission statement? Does this company contribute to their community? What other opportunities are there within this company? What sector or industry is this company in? Who does this company serve, and how does the company serve that customer?

Answering these questions will give you invaluable information about the company. You can then use this information in your cover letter, resumé, and interview. If you want the best chance of getting this job, do your research and know a few extra details about the company.

The job description will tell you who to submit your cover letter and resumé to. It may also include a job number that the company uses to filter applications.

Your cover letter will be the hiring manager's first impression of you and your skills, so you want to make sure you give the employer what they are asking for. If you communicate information that doesn't relate to the job description, then the company will not perceive you as a good match for them.

A job description is like a grocery list of items that an employer is looking for in potential candidates. The more items on their grocery list they can find in a candidate, the better. It is your job to show the employer you have most (not necessarily all!) of the items on their grocery list.

This grocery list makes up their ideal candidate, but they understand that some candidates may not have every requirement. It is acceptable to apply for the job if you do not have every single skill or certification the employer is looking for.

My rule of thumb is if you have 70% of the skills, qualifications, or experience the employer is looking for, then apply!

If you don't review the job description, you won't know the skills to mention in your cover letter. You could list several great skills you possess, but unless you target specific keywords from the job description, this alone will not connect the dots for the employer.

Go ahead and print off the job description you are applying for. Yes, actually print it. Start by looking at the different skills that the employer is looking for in his or her ideal candidate.

If there is a "required" skills or certifications section, you want to include *any* relevant experience you have in your cover letter. If an employer lists a skill twice, it is extremely important to the position.

Choose three to five skills from the job description you feel will be the most important for the job and highlight them. If there are qualifications, certifications, or degrees you need to have for the position, be sure to highlight them.

If you are having a hard time understanding which ones are most important, ask yourself the Who What Where When Why questions to help get you started. What exactly will you be doing in this position? Who will you be helping? What will you be responsible for? By asking yourself these questions about the posting, you should get a good idea of which skills are most important.

———

Job seekers overlook many of the skills they have developed in previous positions. Let's talk about customer service for a moment. Customer service is such a broad term, and you develop all kinds of customer service skills in virtually any role you've ever worked in. This includes working in retail, the fast-food industry, or even volunteering for organizations.

So if you're having a difficult time understanding how your skills relate to the job description, ask yourself—have you taken orders from customers? Have you helped customers find items in a store? Have you received complaints from customers and had to resolve them? What about fulfilling orders for customers to make sure they received the right items, or they received the correct change after paying for something?

Each of these examples is experience and can explain a variety of different skills under the heading of customer experience.

Every difficult conversation with a customer, manager, or supervisor requires us to use communication, negotiation, and professional skills. Times we've handled money in a store, our managers have trusted us to keep accurate transactions. Each role in every job in the world requires us to follow a set of instructions and perform specific tasks. We continually improve using these skills every day.

Be sure to give yourself credit for the skills you have. You're more talented than you think!

———

Capture the hiring manager's attention by capitalizing on three to five skills mentioned in the job description. Skills beyond your top three to five do not deserve to take up real estate on your cover letter.

Job descriptions have been around for years and have done a great job explaining the duties in a position. But, times are changing. Now, employers are searching for new talent by creating job scorecards.

In the next chapter, I'll review what a job scorecard is and how you can use it to land your dream job.

THE JOB SCORECARD_

W HEN I WORKED at the Career Resource Centre at Brock University, it was quite common to see job descriptions that outlined the specific duties of a job. You could easily understand the expected duties of the job and the position requirements, such as school degrees, certifications, and skills.

Since then, there have been major changes in the way companies are finding A-level talent. This has taken the form of job scorecards.

A job scorecard focuses on the purpose, desired outcomes, and competencies required to excel in a position. A job scorecard also includes technical and cultural competencies to ensure all new hires will be in alignment with the existing company culture. Both character and ability are value indicators to determine if you are a good fit for the organization.

While the job description focuses on the duties the employee will perform every day, the job scorecard focuses on the achievements or results from doing such activities. On this scorecard, you will see a list of SMART (Smart, Measurable,

Achievable, Realistic, Timely) outcomes expected in the position.

To put it another way, the job scorecard focuses on outcomes, where a job description lists duties.

Achievement-focused job scorecards allow the company to evaluate if you, as the candidate, can deliver results.

A business owner needs to know their employees are not simply performing duties, but more importantly, achieving results that contribute to the mission and growth of the company. An owner needs to make sure new hires are worth the investment, right?

Companies know it is important to have employees fit not only ability-wise but also in a cultural capacity. When candidates fit the company culture, they will be happier and more loyal to the company's mission. Therefore it's imperative that companies find candidates who fit the company culture as early as possible in the hiring process.

———

Quick example.

Have you heard of some of the interview questions Google asks their candidates? If not, give yourself a break and research some of Google's interview questions. They will blow your mind.

Sometimes Google asks thought-provoking or even outlandish questions. The purpose is to determine if a candidate is a cultural fit. When faced with a difficult or odd question, does the candidate give up easily? Or does the candidate accept the question and prove they will do whatever it takes to succeed?

A company like Google wants outside-the-triangle thinkers, not cookie-cutter thinkers.

The purpose of highlighting Google as an example is so you understand how far companies will go to determine if you'll be a cultural fit with the company. Be honest throughout your job search process, as your unique perspective and character can be exactly what the company is looking for. Being anyone other than yourself will flat-outset you up for failure.

————

When I first saw Self-Publishing School's student success rep job scorecard, I instantly knew Self Publishing School was looking for candidates who fit their culture, and who would provide results. The hiring process with SPS turned out to be one of the most unique and thought-provoking experiences in my employment history.

What did Self-Publishing School *culture* look like?

There are five facets to SPS culture: honesty and integrity, fail fast and fail forward, continuous improvement; everyone is responsible for facilitating change, and best is the standard.

Knowing these cultural values made it easy for me to put 100% into getting this job. It also made it easier for Self-Publishing School to find great talent since they expressed their culture in the job scorecard.

If an applicant knew they wouldn't be a good cultural fit, great! They would not apply. Self-Publishing School didn't need to waste time on this applicant and instead focused solely on attracting and hiring A-level talent.

The second thing I noticed immediately was a focus on results. As my experience would have it, I knew a lot about how to convey my work experiences into results-oriented sentences. This is a skill in itself, and it will help you market yourself better as you are going through different job applications.

Knowing the expected key product indicators of the position put the job into perspective for me. Since I understood the objective of the position (the results), I knew exactly what SPS expected of me once I obtained this position. I could determine whether I had the skill set necessary to excel in the position.

Knowing the expected results of the position set me up for success in the interview. The detail-oriented nature of the job scorecard meant the interviewers would expect the same amount of detail in the interview. I used the information in the scorecard to crush the interview.

Later, I learned there were over 100 people in the applicant pool for this position. I made it to the top 25, then the top five, and was finally selected first overall. It was so empowering, knowing I had made it past every step of the way using the skills I'm sharing with you here.

Reflecting on it now, this was the best interview process I ever experienced. They set expectations from the get-go with a clear focus on results, not only duties. They knew the culture and work ethic they needed to achieve those results.

I knew this was exactly the type of company I wanted to work for, and that motivated me to crush it!

As we move further into the digital era, job descriptions that only list duties and skills are becoming outdated. Job scorecards are more actionable and provide a greater scope of the position and company you'll be working for.

In an era where we expect things at a reduced cost in half the time using half the resources, companies are looking for results—yesterday. Provide the information the employer is looking for when you begin employment relationship and you'll be more likely to land your dream job.

Next, I will explain the format of a cover letter so you can use either the job description or scorecard to build an effective cover letter.

COVER LETTER FORMAT_

A WELL-FORMATTED COVER letter will give your future employer a great first impression of your organizational skills. A badly formatted cover letter will leave whoever ends up reading it with a bad taste in his or her mouth. It's a simple as that.

Since the whole purpose of writing a cover letter and resumé is to land a job, you should put forth the effort to make it perfect. Ignoring these formatting tips may result in someone reviewing your application and throwing it out simply because you lack the organizational ability to communicate your skills.

This can be a hard pill to swallow, but it happens all the time.

First impressions last, and you want to make sure you knock this first impression out of the park. I have a quote I hope will get this point across. It's from one of my favourite TV shows, Suits.

The ultra-savvy, world-class lawyer, Harvey Specter tells his then-naive associate, Mike Ross, "If you start behind the eight-ball, you'll never get in front."

In order to stay in front of the eight ball—and in front of all the other candidates—you need to get ahead of the pack with a kickass cover letter.

A cover letter is a one-page document. No more, no less. It's an opportunity for you to put your work experience into context for your future employer, and therefore, it is more personal than a resumé.

A cover letter's format is straightforward—an introductory paragraph, the main body where you'll communicate your skills, and the closing paragraph. Since the purpose of a cover letter is simple—getting an interview—do not make your cover letter more confusing than it needs to be by adding extra paragraphs or including information that does not belong.

That is it. No extra bells and whistles, no spinning rims, and no Gucci Gang.

Consistent format throughout this document will ensure your information looks professional. Consistency is organized and organized is professional.

Let's put this into context a little bit. Let's say a hiring manager is comparing your cover letter to another candidate's. Your information is well-formatted, easy to read, and organized into three paragraphs on a single page. Meanwhile, the other candidate's cover letter uses a variety of fonts, with jumbled information, and is three pages long.

I promise you this: employers want candidates who efficiently communicate their value. The one page, concise, and effective cover letter will win over the disjointed, three-page document every time.

Great things come in small packages. Quality over quantity. Less is more.

These are philosophies used by uber-successful companies, so take the hint and use these strategies in your application.

Now that you know what to include in your cover letter, along with good formatting techniques, we should discuss a few things you should *not* include in your cover letter (or resumé).

Do not include pictures on your cover letter or resumé. Do not include information regarding marital status, sexual preference, religious affiliations, or political leanings.

Unless necessary for the position you're applying to, these topics do not speak to employment skill or experience. If you're honest about creating a targeted, effective cover letter for the job you're applying to, you need to focus on how you'll provide value to the company.

———

International students applying to work in North America, take note. While other cultures may encourage including pictures and age when applying; this is not a requirement in the North American employment market.

———

Now for the most important part of this "do not include on your cover letter" list.

Do not say how the company will help you advance in your career, or provide you new opportunities to grow. In fact, do not say a single thing about what the company can or will do for you.

This entire process is about how you will provide value for the company, not the other way around.

A hiring manager's sole focus is to hire a candidate with the most experience and skill, and do it efficiently. They're looking for a candidate who will provide results and fill a void in the company's need.

Your goal must be narrow in its focus as you move forward in this process: state you have the experience and skill the company is looking for. Plus, you can provide the results to show it. You are the answer they are looking for.

As soon as you mention what the company can do for you, you've missed the mark. You're not communicating how you can provide value, or providing what the company needs.

If you're focused on getting a job, focus only on how you can provide for the company.

Now we have a solid understanding of a cover letter's format. We know that a well-organized cover letter will leave a great first impression. We know that getting these small details right will put us a step ahead of our competition. Finally, we know a few things we should not include in our cover letter.

Next, I will show you exactly how to write your cover letter. Let's get started so you can get that job!

HOW TO BUILD YOUR COVER LETTER_

IN THE NEXT FEW PAGES, I will show you precisely how to create an effective cover letter for the specific job you want.

You will have so much confidence when you finish because you will know how to target keywords from the job description, and indicate you have the skills the employer is looking for. In other words, you will learn how to set yourself up for success, and to land your dream job.

A cover letter breaks down into four main sections. The first section is the company's contact information. Second is your introductory paragraph. Third is where you will provide context to the skills you have, matching what the employer is looking for. The fourth section is your closing paragraph. Follow this guideline and you will be all set!

Now it's time to create your cover letter. At the top of a new word doc, type the contact information of the company you are applying to, using the details below as a reference.

Company name

The company's street address

City, State/Province, area code

The company's phone number

When you finish, it should look something like this:

Company Name

123 Main Street

Toronto, Ontario, M5V 2T6

123-456-7890

Since you have done research on the company, you'll already know the company's address and who the hiring manager is. Next, you'll want to address your cover letter to that hiring manager. This takes the form of "Attn: Hiring Manager" or "Attn: Michael Lachance".

If you don't know the hiring manager's name, pick up the phone and call the company. Ask who the hiring manager is.

The little things, like using the hiring manager's real name, matter. From a hiring perspective, it shows you've done your research. The hiring manager won't have to ask themselves if you're taking this job search seriously because you've taken initiative by asking who holds that position.

Many candidates do not do their research. Some candidates even put "To whom it may concern."

This is one of the worst things you can do to address the hiring manager. Saying "To whom it may concern" is impersonal. You will stand out if you're the only candidate who doesn't know the hiring manager's name. And not in a good way.

Remember, some companies use programs to filter through the applications they receive. If you don't include the manager's name, he or she is less likely to consider your application.

The second section of your cover letter is the introductory paragraph. It should be only two or three sentences long. In the first sentence, introduce yourself let the employer know what job you are applying to. If there was a job number on the job description/scorecard, include it here.

———

If someone who already works for the company referred you, include his or her name here. Referrals can go a long way when it comes to getting you hired. Take advantage of this!

———

In the second sentence, include one or two skills, certifications, or educational experiences you have that will allow you to exceed in the position. Capture the employer's attention. Give them a reason to continue learning more about you.

In the third sentence, state you have the experience and skills to excel in this position, and make it obvious. Explain how you will benefit the company and bring value to the team.

In the third section, you will target the skills from the job description and explain how your experiences address those needs. Review the job description/scorecard once more and highlight the top three skills or characteristics you think are most important for the position.

I need you to appreciate how important it is to target the skills that the employer is looking for. Without presenting this connection for the employer, you're not showing the employer you are the candidate they need.

Let's imagine you are a baseball player at home plate, ready to take a swing at a pitch. In this analogy, the pitch is the job skill, and you want to connect the pitch with your personal experience and value to hit a home run.

The only way for you to get a home run is to show the employer how you will apply your experience towards the skill they need.

Let's imagine a job description that states the ideal applicant has customer service skills.

To get a home run, you need to show the employer you have customer service skills and how you've used these skills in the past. The employer wants to quickly understand the impact you've had on customers, and I encourage you to use the questions below to get started.

Have you dealt with an irate customer? Did you manage the situation well?

Has a customer ever recognized you, even in passing, from your kind interactions or disposition?

When have you led a team in the workplace to support a customer request?

By answering these questions, you'll explain your customer service experience with context, and in a way the employer understands..

Thank the employer for creating a job description letting us know what specific skills they are looking for. Now, we don't have to guess about what experience to include on our cover letter.

Thanks, employer!

———

This may be the last paragraph the employer will ever read about you, so make sure you have targeted the skills in the job description. If you communicate information that does not relate to what the employer is looking for, then the company will not consider you a good match.

The entire third paragraph needs to focus on the employer's specific needs.

To put this into context, I'd like to share a cover letter I used in my application to the Ontario Provincial Police. Some candidates waited months for an interview with the O.P.P. but I was invited for an interview in only a few weeks. I like to believe having a strong cover letter and resumé was the reason I secured an interview so soon.

———

Police officers interact with civilians all day long, meaning applicants must have strong communication skills. I wanted to make sure I highlighted my communication skills in my cover letter.

My sister and I have grown up around police officers all of our life. We got to see first-hand how police work with the public in all kinds of ways. While most police interactions with the public are rewarding, some experiences can be difficult and demanding.

Adapting to these different scenarios was enticing to me. I have experience in a wide variety of jobs, working with many socio-economic populations, and each provided me with unique experiences.

I had to explain my experience in a few short sentences on my cover letter, and I wanted to use my employment experience as the real hook for this skill.

In my cover letter I wrote:

Five years ago, I began employment with Waterville TG as a labourer. Within a short amount of time, I was promoted to Quality Control Specialist where I represented Waterville across North America. In this role, I minimized quality issues by actively listening to customers, identifying their needs, and implementing countermeasures. My communication skills allowed me to work fluidly with many departments and levels of management.

In only a few sentences, I highlighted my personal and professional development resulting from my communication skills.

You could say that I did a lot of research when it came to learning more about the O.P.P. I wanted to understand the mission statement, values, struggles, and successes in policing communities in Ontario.

After learning the O.P.P. values engaged members of the community, continuous improvement, and continued education, I came out swinging in my cover letter. I did this by stating that within a few years, I went from a manual labourer to Quality Control Specialist—a huge indicator of personal and professional growth.

These statements proved the value I would bring: a desire to constantly improve—a core value of the organization to which I was applying.

The next skill I brought up was communication. This demonstrates proof of past work experiences, not only just saying I have them.

Active listening is an important trait in police work, and I knew if I targeted that skill in my cover letter, I'd demonstrate the results the O.P.P. would appreciate.

I then ended the section by saying I worked and communicated fluidly with many departments and levels of management.

Professionalism is also a strong value of the O.P.P., and I knew my promotions and supervisor experience would speak to this value. I don't simply explain that I was a supervisor, however. I focused on the results of my actions since all employers want to see results from their employees.

Two years ago, I was promoted to Quality Control Laboratory Supervisor. This was a big challenge, as the lab had not been managed before, yet I used this as an opportunity to demonstrate my leadership abilities along with my desire for a challenge. I now supervise over nine lab technicians and have overseen multiple audits with zero non-conformances.

I maintain a theme of constant improvement in my employment positions. Each sentence is results-focused, since I know police officers continually participate in training activities throughout their careers.

I use every sentence as an opportunity to prove I have the experience the O.P.P. desires in applicants. I am showing them I am the missing puzzle piece. Connecting these dots for the employer meant that I secured an interview right away.

———

A single, accurate rifle shot is more effective than a shotgun when targeting skills. You cannot speak to every single skill the employer is looking for. Focus on the skills you have, and the employer is looking for, and present yourself as a match for the employer.

The fourth section of your cover letter is your closing paragraph and it should be three sentences long. Thank the employer for considering your application and mention you hope to hear from them soon. Include your preferred method of communication. Finally, invite the employer to review your resumé.

At the bottom of the page, I suggest typing "Enclosed: Resumé (2)." This tells the employer you have two documents attached to your cover letter.

Completely necessary? Maybe not. But it shows your professionalism and organization skills subtly. And what employer doesn't value these skills? They all do!

To recap, you will begin your cover letter with the company's address. You will then introduce yourself in the first paragraph and state the position for which you are applying. Next, you'll clarify you have the experience the employer is looking for, using concrete examples from your past. You will end your cover letter by thanking the employer for reviewing your cover letter along with your contact information.

To give you an idea what this will look like when you're done, look at my cover letters in the next few pages. Observe how I target specific skills I took from the job description.

In the next chapter, I will have some final suggestions to help you make sure your cover letter is flawless. I'll make sure you've crossed your T's and dotted your I's. You don't want to miss out on these tips!

SAMPLE COVER LETTER.

Police Academy
123 Police Avenue
123-456-7890
policeacademy@gmail.com

December 9, 2015

Attn: Officer Carl, Uniform Recruitment,

It is with confidence and pleasure that I apply for a position of constable with the Ontario Provincial Police. I have demonstrated many of the O.P.P.'s core values in my tenure at Waterville TG and in my role as Quality Control Laboratory Supervisor. I firmly believe my ethical character, employment experience, and life experience make me a strong candidate for a constable position.

Five years ago I began employment with Waterville TG as a laborer. Within a short time I was promoted to a Quality Control Specialist position where I represented Waterville across North America. In this role I minimized quality issues by actively listening to customers, identifying their needs, and implementing countermeasures. My communication skills allowed me to work fluidly with many departments and levels of management. Two years ago, I was promoted to Quality Control Laboratory Supervisor. This was a big challenge as the lab had not been managed before, but I used this as an opportunity to demonstrate my leadership abilities along with my desire for a challenge. I now supervise over nine lab technicians and have overseen multiple audits with zero non conformances. My role also includes document control and ensuring proper testing methods and failed test procedures are followed. Outside of work I have an active social life, play sports in the community, and have sought volunteer opportunities with the Red Cross and Rebound Sarnia-Lambton. All of these experiences have encouraged me to want to make a real and positive impact on my community.

I invite you to view the rest of my resume that provides more information in regards to my employment and volunteer history. I will gladly answer any questions you may have and can be contacted to schedule an interview via email at michance.11@gmail.com or on my cell phone at (123)-456-7890. Thank you for your time and consideration.

Michael Lachance

Enclosed: Resume (2)

FINAL THOUGHTS_

So, you have finished writing your cover letter. Now what?

I hate to say it, but now it's time to do the one thing everyone hates to do. Proofread!

Read your cover letter out loud—not just in your head. When you read it in your head, your brain will automatically correct errors and make sentences flow better than they sound.

If it sounds bad when your future employer reads it, I can guarantee you will not be moving forward in the job-search process.

It is important to remember that the whole purpose of writing a cover letter is to land an employment position. The company is looking to invest their hard-earned business dollars into a candidate. Successful employees create successful businesses, correct?

It bears repeating: Don't explain what the company can do for you in your cover letter and resumé. Instead, everything you put on paper while going through this process should focus entirely on how you can contribute to the company. You are the GIVER, not the TAKER in the entire job search process.

Therefore, you need to repeatedly ask yourself: How will I contribute to the goals and objectives of this company? How will I use my own skills to help this company grow? What skills are most relevant to this position, and how can I maximize the potential I am bringing to the table?

Every sentence you write in your cover letter is an opportunity to show your strengths. Do not miss out on these opportunities. The company is throwing you an entire baseball game's worth of pitches by giving you the job description. Understand the pitch, and use this information to crush some home runs out of the park.

You have now learned what a cover letter is, who needs one, and how to use job descriptions and scorecards to maximize our potential. You know how to format and build a cover letter line by line to sell yourself to your future employer, giving them no other option than to hire you for this job.

Now, it's time to build the tool—your resumé—that you will use to communicate your employment experience in an effective, results-oriented way. An achievement-focused resumé will allow you to show your future employer you are not just a robot performing duties at a job.

Instead, you will show your future employer you are a results-oriented professional, ready to crush any opportunity given to you. Let's dive in.

WHAT IS A RESUMÉ?_

Now that you know how to create a marketable cover letter, it's time to update your resumé. In this chapter, I will explain what a resumé is, the different kinds of resumés, and how we can create a resumé in a way that addresses the employer's needs directly.

While your cover letter is the first document an employer will see when you apply for a job, your resumé will provide a more in-depth look at your employment history. Submit both documents when applying to a job in the form of a job application.

Remember, 98% of people don't make it past the resumé screening when applying for a new job. Since you're reading this book, there's a good chance you're part of this 98%. In this chapter, I'll show you how to improve your resumé in a way that speaks to the employer, and it will significantly increase your chances of being part of the two percent that makes it past resumé screening.

A resumé is your professional business card you can use to

market yourself when applying to jobs. It showcases your employment, education, and volunteer achievements. It is also common to include awards and certifications on a resumé to give employers a rounded picture of who you are as a professional candidate.

In your resumé, it is imperative to write achievement-focused sentences. I'll show you how to write achievement sentences in the next few chapters but for now, let's make sure we understand the difference between an achievement-focused resumé and a resumé that merely lists duties.

An achievement-focused resumé speaks directly to an employer's needs by matching your unique experience and skill with the company's needs. Providing results (or achievements) in your resumé will paint a story of your work ethic to accomplish tasks, provide value, and contribute to the company's bottom line.

Simply listing duties on your resumé does not paint a picture of your work ethic. Listing duties does not make it easy for the hiring manager to understand the value you will bring.

To put it frankly, listing duties will not help you land your dream job.

There are two common kinds of resumés. The first is called Chronological and the second is Functional. Each has their own strengths and weaknesses. I don't want to spend a lot of time diving deep into each one because my method uses the strengths of both. But knowing a little about each may help you choose the best for you depending on the experience you have.

A Chronological resumé lists employment history in reverse chronological order so your most recent work experience comes first and your oldest experience last. Each employment position you list allows you to highlight specific skills, meaning you can focus on keywords from the job description. Your future employer will quickly see the work you've done most recently and how it can apply to the position.

A Functional resumé is a little less common. It lists skills in functional categories such as marketing or project management to create industry-focus in your resumé. This is most beneficial when you have a lot of experience in one specific area—and the company is looking for a candidate with a lot of experience in that one thing.

My method mixes the best elements of both types of resumé and is versatile for individual scenarios.

The biggest mistake you can make on your resumé is only listing the duties you performed at a job. Listing duties does not provide a picture of how you brought value, results, or achievements to the company. Many candidates I've supported in their job search only have duties listed on their resumé because they do not understand what the employer is looking for.

In the next chapter, I will show you how to create achievement-focused sentences and it will transform your resumé for the better. But first, a few more important details before we get there.

It's time to get in the head of an employer.

When the employer picks up your resumé, you need to show you have the experience (education, employment, volunteer, or certifications) necessary to excel in the position. There needs to be an immediate attraction to your application or the hiring manager will throw it to the side and never look at it again.

To maintain a competitive edge in your job search, always strive to improve in the positions you hold by getting promotions. Every one of these promotions will support your credibility in moving up the corporate ladder. Never forget that your actions now will impact how easy or difficult it is to hire you in the future.

Promotions on a resumé show a strong work ethic, professionalism, and leadership. These are the qualities all employers want in their companies.

––––––

Before we move any further, I want to let you in on a little secret. This secret is for those who want to be hired faster and earn promotions sooner. It is not for those who want to stay static in their current positions, and not move up the corporate ladder.

Here's the secret: the more promotions you get in a job, the easier it is to get more promotions down the road—even if it's in another industry.

Companies don't promote people with a lousy work ethic. Companies promote employees who show up and work hard every single day. The employees who make smart decisions, who are great team players, and who encourage those around them, are the ones companies look to for promotions.

Strive to earn promotions in the workplace and to "move up the corporate ladder". Any advancement will show a proven track record of being an ideal employee. No matter where you work now—whether it's at a local coffee shop or an on-campus job—set your sights on a promotion. Getting a promotion now will make it easier for a future employer to hire you.

When a hiring manager sees you've received a promotion or two, they see the commitment and loyalty you have for your employer. They see how the company trusted your judgement and gave you increasing amounts of responsibility. They also see your desire to keep improving since every promotion comes with more responsibility.

Every time you get a promotion, you take on a bigger leadership role, learn the managerial systems that come with it, learn to communicate better, and learn to supervise others—among many other leadership and managerial skills.

These are the skills that will make you a stronger candidate. It sets you apart from the people who have been working for the same length of time but have not risen to the occasion. From a hiring perspective, seeing career advancement on a resumé tells me you have a history of doing what it takes to succeed.

———

Employment and volunteer experience can be relevant as far back as five to 10 years. If you include work experience over 10 years old, make sure it's relevant to the position to which you're applying.

Our economy is well into a major transition from industrial and manufacturing to digital and online industries. For many jobs, experience from ten or fifteen years ago is likely not relevant anymore.

Always keep your resumé current in case a new employment opportunity presents itself. There is nothing worse than having a casual networking opportunity come up, but not having your resumé put together. This can feel like a punch in the gut. From this moment forward, you will be a proactive candidate in your job search.

Finally, some questions to keep in mind as you are building your achievement-focused resumé:

- When have you succeeded in a job?
- Have you failed in a job? If so, what did you learn?
- Do you have well-rounded experience that would entice me to hire you?
- Are you a driven individual? How can you convey that drive to an employer?
- How can you prove these points to your future employer in your resumé?

As we move forward, keep in mind you are building a story for a hiring manager. A resumé can vividly paint this story. There is a beginning and end to every story, and the employer needs to know there were results in the work you've accomplished so far.

Now that we have learned what a resumé is and how we can use it, the different types of resumés, and why it's so important to show advancement in our employment history, it's time to learn a little more about who actually needs a resumé.

I'll give you a hint. You! You need a resumé.

WHO NEEDS A RESUMÉ?_

IN THE PREVIOUS CHAPTER, we discussed what a resumé is, how to use it as an effective job search tool, and the different ways in which we can submit our resumés to potential employers. Now it's time to discuss who actually needs one.

You, along with every other single person looking for a job right now, need a resumé. Not just any resumé—you need to speak to the employer's needs and get you a job, fast.

You owe it to the employer—and yourself—to make hiring you as easy as it can be for all parties involved. Follow my system and you will provide a path of least resistance for the employer.

The first step is to create a new resumé for every single position to which you are applying. This will give you the best odds of getting a job since you are tailoring each resumé to highlight the skills needed for each job. More on this later.

Is this time-consuming? Yes, it can be!

But do you know what's even more time-consuming?

Not taking charge of your employment destiny right now. Every day that goes by without having an effective resumé is another day without a job, another day lost from building a credible employment history.

In the end, you lose time and money, and *ain't nobody got time for that!*

A resumé is a working document. This means you must regularly update it with any new employment-related experiences you gain.

When was the last time you updated your resumé?

Any time you gain a new employment position, certification or award, or educational experience, you need to update your resumé immediately. Do this now and you won't forget to do it in the future.

Be proactive. You don't want to miss any employment opportunity that presents itself.

————

Before moving on, let's be honest with ourselves: how long will resumés even last? And what other resources are out there to help with our job searches?

resumés will be around for a long time—whether it's printed on a few pieces of paper or a file on your computer ready to go out at will. And now, LinkedIn has cemented itself as the next digital step in the modern job search.

If you haven't done so already, take a few minutes and sign up on LinkedIn to create a path of least resistance for your next job search. Employers will be able to find you amongst the sea of other applicants. It also allows head-hunters to proactively find you based on your skills, jobs, accomplishments, and endorsements.

You'll also find relevant job opportunities by following specific job industries or companies you would like to work for down the road. Researching a company's philosophies, interests, and employment opportunities has never been easier than it is on LinkedIn.

———

Do yourself a favour and hand in your resumé in person whenever possible. I know we are moving into the digital age, but showing yourself to the manager of the organization will put a face to the name and that will help you stick out from the crowd.

You will have an advantage over any applicant that didn't hand their resumé in person.

With that being said, a lot of companies only accept digital applications. Organizations are using every opportunity to cut costs and increase efficiency, so they will use any opportunity to avoid sucking endless manpower into hiring a candidate.

Research how the company you're applying to wants to receive applications. Follow their instructions one step at a time.

———

Many job industries are going strictly digital, including police services, such as the Ontario Provincial Police. Rather than collecting cover letters and resumés, school transcripts, reference letters, awards and certificates, drivers' licenses and birth certificates on paper, they now request these documents submitted electronically. The idea that you *need* to submit cover letters and resumés in person, on paper, is no longer true.

———

To put it plainly, the trend from personal to digital experience continues to infiltrate every part of our lives, including the modern job search.

In the next chapter, we'll be looking at how to format your resumé. Use these tips to create a resumé of employment excellence, and you will open doors to new opportunities in ways you never thought possible.

From this moment on, you can put your brain on autopilot and enjoy the ride. Don't worry—I'm a very experienced driver and will get you to your destination safely!

This ride starts with formatting your resumé. Let's get started.

RESUMÉ FORMAT_

IN THIS CHAPTER, you will learn how to format your resumé properly. A good format will give your future employer a great first impression of your professional work ethic since so many people overlook basic formatting.

I can't tell you how many resumés I've reviewed and thought the candidate's work ethic would be sloppy based on his or her unorganized (and badly formatted) resumé.

This is a big reason why 98% of people don't make it past resumé screening. Fair or unfair, first impressions last.

A well-formatted resumé shows strong organizational skills—a great attribute to show your employer as early as possible in this new relationship. It also means your resumé will be easy to read, allowing the employer to see how you'd be a good fit for the company.

The employer will view you as an effective communicator from the first glance at your resumé.

Now what, you might ask, do I mean when I refer to consistent formatting?

Consistent formatting means the font you use, the heading sizes you choose, and indentation placements are the same throughout your entire resumé. All job titles and text sections should be bolded consistently and the same size. All dates aligned to the far-right side of the page.

Consistency in every section of your resumé is key. This is the most overlooked, yet most impactful improvement you can make to your resumé right now.

Inconsistent formatting is the most common shortcoming I see on resumés and, overall, it gives me a bad impression regarding your organizational skills. I know many of these suggestions are small details—but that's what makes them important. A resumé is a professional document and if you can't organize this document professionally, how can an employer trust the quality of your work once they hire you?

On the other hand, format your resumé correctly, and you set expectations that this is the way you will approach your new position at the company.

Again, first impressions last!

Every job title, font and size, employment date position, and every break in the resumé needs to be the exact same. This means that when you bold your first job title under Work Experience, you need to bold every other job title, too. If the job title is size-12 Times New Roman font, then every job title needs to be the same size and font. If you're using circle bullet points, then every bullet point needs to be consistent.

Creating headers to distinguish between different sections of your resumé is a must. The best way to break up the sections of your resumé is by bolding, underlining, and caps lock each of the section headings.

Bolding a new word or underlining a title creates a visual break for the reader. Whoever is reading your resumé will know there is a clear separation between your work experience, volunteer experience, and awards. Better yet, use the Styles function of your word processor to apply the correct style using header tags.

A resumé usually contains these sections listed in this order, depending on your experience:

- Header with name and contact information
- Education section
- Employment Experience section
- Volunteer Experience section
- Awards or Certifications section
- References

———

Although it would be nice to see your personality shine through your resumé by adding your picture or a few friendly emojis, do not include them. This is a professional document meant to entice a hiring manager to take you on to his or her team. Typically, North American industries don't request, want, or need this information.

Hiring a new candidate is a tedious and time-consuming endeavour—a hiring manager will ask themselves if you have the skills, the drive, the passion, and characteristics that would allow you to fit into the company culture seamlessly.

Don't detract from your professional value by including emojis or other irrelevant information.

———

I can't stress how important formatting is, so I want to give you a final tip. I put my dates to the far-right side of the page beside every employment position. This is something you need to take time to do.

Some may argue that this is silly, tedious, is not important, and that no one will notice if there is a few spaces to the right of your date (meaning it is not completely aligned to the right-hand side of the page). Don't be this person!

Take the time to push the dates to the far-right side of the page.

If a hiring manager has two resumés in front of him, trying to decide who to move forward with, I have a strong feeling he will choose the one who took a few minutes to make sure to take care of the small details. After all, a hiring manager wants to hire someone with a detail-oriented work ethic, right?

Show the hiring manager you pay attention to these small details and that you'll bring the same work ethic to their organization.

Try to keep your resumé down to two pages. If your resumé is three pages long, skim through your work experiences and find something to remove. Maybe you have sentences that don't speak to the most important skill you need for the job.

Perhaps there is an employment experience that is not relevant to the position you are applying to at all. Having a third page (especially if you're only using half of the third page) leaves an unfulfilled feeling.

Finally, keep track of updates to your resumé by naming your job application files correctly. Since you will always be updating your resumé with new experiences, name the document so you know what resumé to pull out for different job applications.

I suggest you name your resumé files like this:

Last name, First name—resumé June 2018.

This way, I know the latest update to this resumé was in June of 2018. I should update my information to reflect all my work experiences, volunteering, awards, and certificates up to this date.

Doing this highlights your organizational skills to your future employer. I can promise you that few people think to edit the file name. Most file names are a random assortment of characters and don't clarify what the file contains. I'm sure I'm not the only one, but it makes it a lot easier for me to open a file if I know what's inside.

Another way you can name your resumé file is by the job you are applying to. This makes it more relevant to different skills you are highlighting in this resumé as opposed to specific dates. Instead of including a date, you could include the industry your resumé speaks to.

You now understand the importance of a properly formatted resumé and the context behind why it is so important. First impressions last, and understanding the techniques in this chapter will allow you to create a resumé your future employer will love.

Let's get started on building your resumé in the next chapter. Present your information in a clear, organized way that will allow your future employer to quickly find the information they are looking for.

HOW TO MAKE A RESUMÉ_

I WILL NOW SHOW you how to create an effective resumé that'll help you make it past resumé screening. Remember, employers disqualify 98% of candidates after reviewing their resumé. I've seen enough resumés to know why, and I can say with confidence that your resumé is missing one of the following suggestions.

The following suggestions come from hundreds of resumés I've reviewed. I've seen great resumés, and I've seen some pretty rough ones. But once you've seen as many resumés as I have, you learn the common traits of strong and poor resumés. I encourage you to use each example I provide for the most effectiveness in your job search.

Let's start from the beginning. Write your contact information at the top of your resumé. Outline your name, home address, email address, and phone number neatly. If you want to get this job, you need to make it as easy as possible for an employer to reach out to you.

I've copied a sample to show you how to organize your

contact information. Pay careful attention to the use of bolded text, alignment to the centre of the page, and the separation line to give the "Header" look we are going for.

Michael Lachance
Street Address, City, Province/State, Area Code
Cell: (123) 456-7890 Email: michance.11@gmail.com

———

Your name should stand out and grab the employer's attention, front and centre. Provide everything the employer will need to contact you.

Two of the biggest mistakes you can make here are not providing adequate contact information and providing it in a disorganized and cluttered manner. No hiring manager wants to take more than a few seconds to know how to get in touch with you.

The next section in your resumé is the Education section. Create a visual break for the reader by bolding and underlining the word Education in all caps. Underneath this header, list your most recent (and relevant to the position you're applying to) degrees.

First, type the degree you hold first and bold the text. Include the date range of when you received this degree and align it to the far-right side of the page. Underneath, in bulleted, standard font, include the university, college, or high school you have graduated from, including the city and state or province.

Your future employer will ask themselves the simple question, "Does this candidate have the degree I need and experience that comes with it or not?" In general, your degree is more important than the school you went to, so put that first.

This is how your education section should look:

EDUCATION

Bachelor of Arts, History   2008–2012

◦ Brock University, St. Catharines, ON

————

The most overlooked and under-utilized organizational tool I've seen on resumés is the date range format.

Most candidate's date alignment is very inconsistent and disorganized. Having some dates aligned to the right-hand side and some not, some beside your degree and some underneath looks very unprofessional.

You may not think something this small could be important, but we are trying to create the best first impression we can for our future employer.

The purpose of creating a resumé is to convince an employer to hire you, right?

Make sure every single date on your resumé, whether it be under education, work experience, volunteering, awards, or certificates are all pushed to the right-hand side of the page.

I studied at the university from 2008 through 2012, so I physically aligned this date range to the far-right edge of the page.

This small formatting tip will make your resumé look highly

organized and professional. Control the controllables and align those dates to the right edge of the page!

———

The next section in your resumé will be Employment Experience.

Employers need to know if your employment experience will prove valuable to their needs. Your job is to prove that you are the candidate they need to hire.

Start by listing your position title first and bold it. Include the date range to the far right edge of the page. Underneath, bulleted in standard font, write the name of the company you worked for. Next to this, include the city and state (or province) of the company's location.

Here is a sample for reference:

EMPLOYMENT EXPERIENCE

Student Success Representative March 2018–Present

San Francisco, California

• Achievement Sentences.

———

Ninety-eight percent of candidates don't create a bridge between their value to what the employer needs. They'll list performed duties but not the achievements or results of their actions.

For example, a candidate will say they have a skill, but not how they used it during employment. Or how they performed a task without stating how that task brought value to the company or customer.

These candidates use terminology people outside their industry will never understand. They fail to communicate how their skills would apply to the job they're applying to.

At the end of the day, the employer does not understand how the candidate will contribute to their needs.

Based on the many resumés I've reviewed, this is the biggest reason 98% of candidates don't make it past resumé screening.

Moving forward, your goal is to laser-focus on the employer's needs. First, identify how your experience contributes to their needs. Second, highlight the value you'll bring to that need using achievement sentences.

Show how you will provide value to the company by writing achievement sentences.

———

Below is an effective system to create achievement sentences. Every sentence underneath your Employment and Volunteer experience should follow this format. The verb is always in the past tense as an achievement is something you have completed or achieved in the past.

Action word (what you did) + **context** (who you did it for) + **achievement** (what you achieved)

In my experience, most candidates only write the first or

second piece of this equation. They state their action word, or what they did in their job. Some candidates go as far as saying who they did it *for*. But there is no result or achievement.

To help you understand the value you provide, ask yourself: why are you doing this action in the first place? Who are you helping by doing this action? What value do you provide and to whom? How does this improve the customer's experience? In what way do you help the company grow and gain more business?

Each achievement sentence should focus on a skill from the job description.

Here are a few samples for you.

Student Success Representative March 2018–Present

Self-Publishing School, San Francisco, California

• Provided email and chat support to students, ensuring their success going through any of Self-Publishing School's programs

• Developed onboarding metrics to measure and report student success rates

• Screened over 450 applications for a Student Success Coach position resulting in two A-Player coworkers who continue to drive growth in the company

• Received the "Playbook Beast Q4 - 2018" award, recognizing my efforts to systematize daily procedures and activities

———

As you can see, I didn't make a vague, blanket-statement like, "emailed students." This does not show a result or achievement. Instead, there is a purpose of emailing our students. It was to ensure their overall success going through the program. At the end of the day, I am making customers happy.

Let's break down the equation once more.

Action word (what you did) + **context** (who you did it for) + **achievement** (what you achieved).

Provided (action word) email and chat support to students (context), ensuring their success going through any of Self-Publishing School's programs (achievement).

Developed (action word) onboarding metrics (context) to measure and report student success rates.

Screened (action word) over 450 applications for a Student Success Coach position (context) resulting in two A-Player coworkers who continue to drive growth in the company (achievement).

Received (action word) the "Playbook Beast Q4 - 2018" award (context), recognizing my efforts to systematize daily procedures and activities.

I provided value in each achievement sentence as my actions resulted in an achievement. A hiring manager will read my resumé and see the results I've provided in the past. I'm giving them exactly what they're looking for.

Repeat this process for all of your employment experiences.

The fourth section of your resumé will be Volunteer Experience. Include any volunteer experience you have in this section, especially if it relates to the job you're applying to.

———

Volunteering is not only admirable, but it can paint a powerful picture on your resumé. It's a great way to show you love to give back to your community and make a positive impact in people's' lives.

If you have zero work experience, or you are looking for other ways to strengthen your resumé, volunteer! Volunteering can add so much value to your resumé you would otherwise not have—including references for employers.

Volunteer and develop skills the company is looking for. Then, build achievement sentences around those skills for your resumé.

———

The Volunteer Experience section will look a lot like your Employment Experience section. First, bold the volunteer position title you held. Align the date range of when you volunteered to the far-right side of the page. The name of the organization and city will go underneath. Then write your achievement sentences.

Follow the same achievement sentence structure:

Action word (what you did) + **context** (who you did it for) + **result** (what you achieved)

Here is another sample for you:

. . .

VOLUNTEER EXPERIENCE

Choices Program Volunteer   March 2018–May 2018

Volunteer Organisation, City, Province/State

• Developed relationships with local youth who had trouble with the law to offer support around making healthy choices

Developed (**action word**) a relationship with local youth who had trouble with the law (**context**) to offer support around making healthy choices (**achievement**).

The fifth section on your resumé, Professional Development, is where you put any awards and certificates you have. Employers don't want to hire robots—they want character and skill! Professional Development is the perfect spot to show what kind of person you are inside and out of the workplace.

Any training relevant to your future employer will go here. Professional certifications, aptitude tests, language tests, extracurricular or volunteer awards, publications, community awards. Heck, include sports awards to reveal what kind of person you are.

Here is the Professional Development section of my resumé. I include the date I was certified on the far-right side of the page.

PROFESSIONAL DEVELOPMENT

Copywriting Mastery - Digital Marketer HQ 2018

Student Success TedX Talk - Presentation Training . . 2010

Career Assistant Training 2010

AWARDS

Facilitating Change Award - Self-Publishing School . 2019

Playbook Beast Q4 - 2018. 2018

Honesty & Integrity Award- Self-Publishing School . 2018

———

Now you are at the end of your resumé. The last line of your resumé will be a single line:

References Available Upon Request.

That's it. You're almost done!

Before you apply to your dream job, create a list of three people you can depend on to give you a positive character reference.

A character reference is someone who can speak to the hiring manager about your character.

To break it down further, a professional reference is someone you have worked with who can speak to your character in the workplace.

A personal reference is someone who knows you outside of any work environment. This is someone who has seen your abilities outside of work. They can vouch for you and the value you bring and can describe your personality.

There are some people you should avoid using as a character reference: your parents, as there may be an obvious conflict of interest, or your best friends. If your parent is your boss or supervisor, find someone else within the organization to speak to your skills.

If you have no reference at all, get out and volunteer!

Most employers will want to see at least three references. Have your references ready before the employer even asks to show how prepared you are.

The employer will need to know how to contact your references. On a new page, write the word "References" and centre it on the page. Write your reference's name and underneath, include the following information:

• Position title, with the company's name

• Phone number

• Email address

• Relationship to reference (personal or professional)

––––––––

Bold each reference's name so it is easy to pick out. This will also establish a visual break between your list of references.

There you have it! You now know how to create a kickass resumé that'll help you land your dream job. With these tips at your disposal, I know you'll be part of the two percent that makes it past resumé screening.

Since you've made such a good cover letter and resumé, I just know you'll get an interview. That's why I've included an entire section on how to prepare for your interview, even providing sample questions to help you prepare.

Let's take a look.

SAMPLE RESUMÉ.

Michael Lachance

Address, City, State/Province, Postal/Zip Code
Cell: (123) 456-7890 Email: ineedajob@gmail.com

EDUCATION

Bachelor of Arts History   2008 - 2012
* Brock University, St. Catharines, ON

EMPLOYMENT EXPERIENCE

Student Success Representative   March 2018 - Present
Self-Publishing School, San Francisco, California
* Provided email and chat support to students, ensuring their success going through any of Self-Publishing School's programs
* Developed onboarding metrics to measure and report student success rates
* Screened over 450 applications for a Student Success Coach position resulting in two A-Player candidates who continue to drive growth in the company
* Received the "Playbook Beast Q4 - 2018" award, recognizing my efforts to systematize daily procedures and activities

Quality Control Lab Supervisor   January 2016 - Present
Waterville TG, Petrolia, ON
* Trained and supervised over nine lab technicians on three separate shifts to ensure proper quality control measures are adhered to
* Audited the quality control lab on a regular basis to verify lab jigs and other quality equipment matches control plans and customer specifications
* Developed operating and troubleshooting instructions for lab technicians to ensure technicians could problem solve on their own before escalating any concerns

Quality Control Specialist   October 2013 – January 2016
Waterville TG Group, Petrolia, ON
* Provided support and training to production team members in the interpretation of product quality, fit and functions
* Managed external customer complaints by investigating concerns and implementing countermeasures/revising PFMEA's with quality engineers
* Maintained quality documentation, improved standard operating procedures for quality, and participated in daily meetings to ensure WTG met customer quality specifications
* Revised control plans on a regular basis to ensure Ford, Honda, Toyota and GM parts conformed to customer specifications and engineering standards
* Developed, revised and distributed Inspection Methods and Operation Standard documents specific to each customers' requirements

Michael Lachance

Address, City, State/Province, Postal/Zip Code
Cell: (123) 456-7890 Email: ineedajob@gmail.com

Quality Control Auditor   July 2013 - October 2013

Waterville TG Group, Petrolia, ON

- Assisted in the Quality Control department to ensure that parts conformed to strict customer specifications on all active shifts
- Coordinated with supervisors, production managers and line operators to clearly explain customer expectations/concerns and suggested corrective actions to limit defect flow-out
- Enforced a Kaizen philosophy by always looking for more efficient ways of producing quality parts in an efficient manner

Senior Career Assistant   May 2011 – April 2012

Career Services, Brock University, St. Catharines, ON

- Developed resources including a Career Paths for Teachers binder which allows students to find career-related information specific to their program
- Worked collaboratively with the Resource Coordinator and Faculty Liaison to plan, coordinate, and deliver career related projects and events for the academic year
- Facilitated weekly meetings and managed daily email and walk-in statistics to ensure our service-goals were met on a weekly and monthly basis
- Presented a workshop on a job-search database called Goinglobal (and many more resources) which significantly enhanced my oral communication skills in front of large audiences while also introducing students and alumni to job related resources
- Interviewed students applying for Career Assistant positions and made recommendations for new hires, while also ensuring their continued success by mentoring new coworkers

PROFESSIONAL DEVELOPMENT/WORKSHOPS

Copywriting Mastery - Digital Marketer HQ	2018
Student Success TedX Talk - Presentation Training	2018
Career Assistant Training	2010

AWARDS

Facilitating Change Award - Self-Publishing School	2019
Playbook Beast Q4 - 2018	2019
Honesty & Integrity Award - Self-Publishing School	2018

References Available Upon Request.

PREPARING FOR THE INTERVIEW_

Now that you have a cover letter and resumé that will get you past resumé screening, it's time to prepare for your interview so you can land your dream job!

Before we move further, I want to tell you the philosophy my dad, Mitch, has pounded into my head over the years.

This philosophy is called the seven Ps. While he used it a lot when coaching me in hockey—the philosophy of the seven P's is for life itself. The seven P's are:

Proper Prior Planning Prevents Piss Poor Performance.

No doubt my dad read this from somewhere, but he does live by it. The seven P's are so important to success. Proper prior planning will prevent you from having a piss poor performance.

It's never too early to prepare for your interview. In fact, why not start right now!?

The best way to land your dream job is to not have a piss-poor interview. The problem is that people do not prepare for their interviews nearly as much as they should. When the day comes, Peter Procrastinator ends up feeling stressed and anxious because he has not prepared.

The answer to this crisis of interview unpreparedness is easy: prepare!

There is a handful of questions you can prepare for that apply to almost any interview. Answering these questions will give you confidence during the rest of the interview.

Answering questions effectively in your interview will prove you have strong communication skills. Struggling to answer questions in the interview means the hiring manager will question your ability on the job.

Follow the seven Ps and I guarantee you will stand out from the pack, even if your education and work experience don't.

How can you properly prepare prior to participating in this potentially positive affair? It's easier than you might think. It all comes down to preparation!

Just like you anticipate problems in the workplace, you need to anticipate interview questions. Questions like, what are your strengths? What are your weaknesses?

These questions should be so easy to answer it should feel like you're taking candy from a baby.

I have asked and been asked this question many times in interviews. You have not properly planned if you're unable to answer this question immediately. You will have a piss-poor interview.

Start thinking about how you can answer this question. Your answers should focus on the employer's needs. If the company is looking for a team player, then speak to a strength you have working as a team.

Communicating your weaknesses can be a little trickier. You don't want to outright state you are terrible at a specific task or mention you have no experience using a skill the employer needs most.

Instead, state a weak skill you posses, but, more importantly, how you've taken action to improve that skill. If you prepare this answer properly, you'll be able to turn your weakness into a strength.

By now, you may ask, *"How the heck can I anticipate questions for a job I've never worked at?"*

Great question!

The first thing I suggest you do is Google it. It's 2018, isn't it? Start by searching, "What questions are asked at a job interview for [insert company name]?" I guarantee you someone else has asked this same question.

Second, I suggest you review the three to five major skills you pulled from the job description. If these skills were important enough to be in the job description, you can bet your bottom dollar they will be discussed during the interview.

At the end of every interview, you'll be asked if you have any questions for the company. Prepare at least two questions you will ask the employer. This is a great opportunity to learn more about the company and exhibit your interest in the position.

Ask about the company's philosophy and values. Ask what an

average day looks like at the company or what promotional opportunities exist.

Not having a question prepared leaves you, the candidate, with a lost opportunity to learn more about the company. Do yourself a favour and create some questions to ask the interviewers.

I promise you, interviewers will see your enthusiasm for the job if you have questions prepared for them.

One final note about interviews before we move on. The goal of the interview is to bring talent onto the company's team. They will not waste time with trick questions or purposely stump you.

So try not to be nervous. Be yourself. Answer the questions honestly. Admit when you don't meet the criteria of what they are looking for. If you are a driven and competent individual, you may get away with not having a few qualifications if you fit the company culture.

Admit where you are weak, over-deliver where you are strong, and you will be victorious.

By doing this kind of proper prior planning, you will certainly not have a piss-poor performance.

Your purposeful preparation will make you a perfect applicant for this position. Let's pitter patter, pal!

INTERVIEWSTREAM_

You NEED to prepare for your interview. Go into it well-versed and articulate your work experiences. Tell the interviewer why you are the best candidate. No—the *only* candidate worthy of consideration.

You'll need answer questions efficiently and effectively. The most impactful way to do this is by practising in an environment similar to a real interview.

InterviewStream is an online tool that sets you up in a mock, online interview. An avatar asks questions and your webcam records your responses. After you answer a few questions, you can go back and review your responses and find areas to improve upon.

You may feel silly while speaking to yourself on webcam, all alone. That's okay. I know how it feels because I have used InterviewStream many times myself. But, the sooner you shake off the self-analysis and self-criticism, the better.

Go to https://interviewstream.com and the next few steps are pretty self-explanatory. Click on Interview Prep and sign up as either a Job Candidate/Student. You can choose to answer specific questions or have random questions generated.

Having a resource like InterviewStream—where you can do mock interviews in the comfort of your own home—is a gift for the modern job seeker. And the fact that you can do this in your bedroom while no one else is around is empowering.

So, stop reading this book right now and go record yourself answering a minimum of five questions. You will promptly understand what questions you are strong at answering and what questions you need to improve upon. Don't wait until your interview before you test yourself under self-imposed pressure.

Seriously—do not skip this step. If you play any sports, you will understand the importance of practising before a game. At practise, you put yourself into situations you will face during a real game to build strong, natural habits. You learn how respond to different situations and gain an awareness of how different scenarios can play out.

Practising gives you strength during games.

Luckily for you, most candidates don't practise. They think they know the answers. They believe they can perform on the spot when the time comes. Or they simply don't take this process seriously.

In the end, this person will lose to the candidate who prepared. The candidate who articulates their experience and value gets the job.

After recording yourself on InterviewStream, watch the video and evaluate yourself.

The first thing to evaluate is what you are communicating.

Are you responding to questions with the skills from the job scorecard? Are you speaking to the skills you highlighted in your cover letter and resumé?

If not, try practising again. The company wants a candidate who has the specific skills listed on the job description or job scorecard. You need to speak to these in skills in the interview, so if you're not doing this on InterviewStream, try again.

As you continue to observe your responses, note the following:

- Body posture
- Body language
- How many times you say "Um" or "Uh"
- Tone of voice

Your posture can say a lot about you. As much as possible, sit up straight. It shows confidence. Plus, an interview is no place for slouching.

Listen for how many times you say um or uh. Saying um or uh is very distracting and unnecessary. Instead of saying um or uh, take a second to collect your thoughts. A five-second break to collect your thoughts is a lot better than you saying uh every now and again.

Tone is important. Employers want to see confidence, character, and excitement from you. Why would they want to hire a monotone robot? Put some excitement in your voice while you practise! Show the company the excited tone you'll bring to the position after you're hired.

Be conscientious of your breathing habits. I've seen many

candidates get anxious during an interview. Their breathing quickens and soon, they are out of breath as they try and answer a few questions. Learning how to control your breathing will go miles in helping you rock this interview.

Now that you have a better understanding of how to prepare in an interview environment, let's discuss specific questions you can prepare for.

TYPES OF INTERVIEW QUESTIONS_

INTERVIEWSTREAM WILL HELP IMPROVE your communication techniques and body language. Now, you'll need some questions to prepare for. The more intelligent your response to a question, the better your odds of landing your dream job.

In this chapter, we will cover some of the most common questions asked in an interview. If you can answer these questions effectively, you will be miles ahead of your competition.

Trust me—few people can answer these questions as coherently as you might think.

More times than I care to admit, I've asked a question the candidate was unprepared for. They stammer, incoherently, providing few actionable details about their employment experience.

I don't want you to make the same mistakes.

These candidates could have been incredible employees. But being unprepared for a few simple questions told me they were unorganized. They didn't prepare for the interview seriously enough.

How can you prepare more effectively? Repeatedly ask yourself why this company should hire you instead of another candidate. What is it about you that would provide the most value for what the company needs?

This can be a tough question since we typically don't enjoy marketing ourselves and our skills. The thing is—that's exactly what you need to do here.

Every sentence you speak must provide value and insight to your skills. Every answer you give will be rated and judged against other candidates.

Unfortunately, an interview is also an opportunity for you to tell an employer why they should not hire you. Therefore, do not bring up experiences that do not relate to the job description or speak to the company's mission, goals, and objectives.

In order for you to maximize the value of your responses, use the STAR method. This method is very effective and breaks down as follows:

Star: describe the Situation

Task: describe the Task required of you

Action: describe the Action you took

Result: describe the Results of your actions

First, you will describe the problem or situation you were facing. Next, you will explain the task, or what you had to do to correct the situation. You will then explain the actions you took to make the change happen. Finally, you will describe the results of your actions.

Notice how this process is similar to how we build achievement sentences?

This method communicates your experience in a way the employer will understand. It also keeps the results of your actions at the front of your mind throughout the interview.

There are two different kinds of interview questions for which you should prepare. Don't get caught up in trying to understand the differences between the two. The key here is to know different types of questions exist, and the approach to answering them is slightly different.

The first kind is a behavioural-based question. Behavioural-based questions highlight your strengths and weaknesses by asking about past behaviours. Past behaviours indicate future behaviours. These details will help the employer understand the value you'll bring to the company.

Keep in mind there is no right or wrong answer to these questions. Rather, the employer is looking for specific examples of how you've performed in the workplace.

Now let's check out some sample behavioural-based questions.

1. Give an example of a time you faced conflict while working as part of a team.
2. Describe a time you had difficulty building a relationship.
3. Have you ever made a mistake? How did you handle it?
4. Give an example of a time you had to take on the role of a leader.

5. Tell me about a time you worked effectively under pressure.
6. Describe a time you didn't meet the expectations of your manager.
7. Have you experienced stressful situations and how did you deal with it?
8. Share an example of how you were able to motivate employees or co-workers.
9. Have you ever gone beyond the call of duty? If so, how?
10. How do you go about prioritizing tasks each day?

For each question, prepare stories about behaviours from your past. Even if you're not asked these specific questions, you'll have several stories prepared that you can speak to in the interview.

The second type of interview question is the competency-based interview question. These questions determine if you have the experience and skill for the job you're applying for.

For these questions, you'll need a solid understanding of the skills the employer is looking for. Think of the different times, experiences, jobs, and environments you've used the skills the employer is looking for. This way, you can speak directly to these skills while answering competency-based questions.

Use the STAR method when answering these questions:

1. Give an example of a time when you led a team. What did you accomplish?

2. Describe a time you've used effective time management to complete a project.

3. Tell me about a time you failed to complete a project on time.

4. Tell me about a time your communication skills helped improve a situation.

5. How do you respond to customer feedback?

6. Describe a situation where you had to deal with an angry customer.

7. What big decision have you made recently? How did you go about it?

8. What is your biggest achievement?

9. Describe a time you've led a team in the past. What did you achieve?

10. Give an example of a time you've identified a new approach to a workplace problem.

If you can answer these questions effectively, you will be miles ahead of the competition. Practise answering these questions the same way as any other professional: repetition.

Professional athletes, police officers, soldiers—you name it. They never stop training. If you genuinely want to land your dream job, practise, and then practise some more.

If you want this job, take practising seriously. Otherwise, you will lose out to the candidate who took the time to practise before the big game.

I have now equipped you with practise interview questions to help you prepare. You understand the types of questions you will need to answer, and now have many examples of questions you can use to prepare for your interview. You also have an effective, results-focused method to answer these questions.

Next, I want to show you how you can prepare even further to truly live by the seven Ps. Let's talk about what you should and shouldn't wear to your interview.

DRESS TO IMPRESS_

THIS CHAPTER IS all about what you should (or should not!) wear to your interview.

I have my own philosophy on what to wear. My philosophy is simple.

Look good. Feel good. Play good.

This is a motto I have stood by for most of my life.

Here is my theory behind *Look good, Feel good, Play good*:

Every time you get dressed up nice and fancy, you feel like a rock star, right?

Like when you get ready for a wedding. The gents spend extra time shaving until their face is as smooth as a baby's bottom. Ladies spend most of the morning in the bathroom doing makeup, getting their hair done and those nails did.

At the end of all this, we look good enough to strut down the red carpet. A bunch of badasses, right? We look good!

When we look good, we feel good.

Think back to the last time you were at a wedding. Everyone at a wedding has an extra boost of confidence, right? An extra pep in their step, some extra swagger in their . . . strut? We're surrounded by a bunch of great-looking people with big smiles, and excitement is all around us.

So, what does that mean? It means we feel good!

When we feel good, we play good.

We have more confidence in these moments not only because we are celebrating marriage, but because we have put ourselves in that positive mindset. When we look our best, we project happiness with our body language. Dressed for success, we are on our A-game.

We know we look our best, so when we see a cute girl or guy, we confidently strut right up and ask for a dance. You dance like no one's watching, using moves you didn't even know you had. This is what I mean by you play good.

This same attitude comes into play when you prepare for an interview. Build that confidence before you even walk into the interview. *Look good, Feel good, Play good.*

My rule of thumb is dress for the job you want. If you are applying for an entry-level position but you really want that supervisor job, dress as if you are applying for that supervisor job. Every interaction with the employer is an opportunity to display your deep desire for this job.

To get a little more specific, the minimum standard is business casual. It is always better to be overdressed than underdressed.

So, what does business casual mean exactly?

Business casual does not mean dressing casually as the name may sound. Instead of thinking business casual means dressing up in a casual outfit (say jeans and a collared shirt), it actually means dressing down a business outfit (suit pants with no tie). The goal is to look professional, put together, and neat.

Whatever you wear to your interview, you are foreshadowing the effort you'll bring to the company and customers.

Your clothes should be clean and wrinkle-free. Men can wear dress or khaki pants with a pair of black or brown loafers (these are good colours to have since they can match pretty much anything). Tuck your shirt in, buttoned up except for the neck.

Use your best judgement for a tie. If you're applying to an industry like law enforcement or the financial industry, a tie is highly encouraged. Otherwise, it may not be necessary.

Be well-groomed. Shave your face, cut, wash, and comb or style your hair. First impressions matter here, too.

Do not wear jeans (no matter how nice they look), running shoes or sneakers, v-necks or casual t-shirts. At minimum, wear a polo.

If you are having trouble picking out an outfit, type "business casual" for men or women into Google. You'll see tons of examples. Google images will do a way better job showing you how to dress business casual than I could ever explain to you in a book.

For women, this also means clean and wrinkle-free clothes. A simple button-down shirt should be a staple item in your closet, often with dress pants and collared shirt or blouse.

Conservative colours work well in interviews. A shoe with a modest heal (kitten heels or Mary Janes) is acceptable, but avoid open-toe shoes. Keep embellishments such as bling, buckles, or studs to a minimum.

When it comes to pants, wear a neutral shade of dress pants or a knee-length skirt with a blazer.

Do not wear low cut shirts, spaghetti strap (or strapless for that matter), denim, or yoga pants, flip flops, sandals, or open-toe shoes.

Wait until after the interview to add your personality into your style of dress. Show off your true style when you know it will be appropriate, when there is no risk to you not getting an interview.

In this chapter, I've shown you how to dress to impress. You will break necks and cash checks with your business casual style.

In the next few pages I will things you should bring to your interview. This will make sure you are prepared for anything that comes your way.

WHAT TO BRING_

Now that we know how to dress for the interview, it's time to learn what we should bring to it.

There is not a whole lot you need to bring to an interview other than a killer mentality, confidence, business casual dress, a strong cover letter and resumé, and a smile to light up the room. That's not too much to ask, is it?

Remember, an interview isn't intended to confuse or intimidate you. The company is searching for someone who will bring value to its team. They want you to be as prepared as you can be.

Employers will request you bring any documents in the interview invitation. If they didn't request anything of you in the interview invitation then they do not expect you to bring anything. With that said, don't be afraid to ask the hiring manager what to bring if you are unsure. It never hurts to ask.

One thing is for sure: if the hiring manager asks you to bring something, you better bring it.

In some industries you may need to bring formal ID, including your drivers' licence and birth certificate. You might need a copy of your cover letter and resumé, a high school or university transcript. A portfolio of artwork or writing would be more common in the arts industry. Any documents that will allow you to back up your work experience with proof.

Items you can choose to bring include a pen and pad of paper, a list of references, and a list of questions to ask the interviewers.

I highly suggest you bring at least one question. Having a question (or a list of questions!) prepared for the interviewers will show just how much you want this job. This is a great way to stand out from the competition.

First, it demonstrates you are an organized professional who thinks ahead. You are not one to leave landing your dream job to chance; you will not miss out on an opportunity to prove, in person, how badly you want this job.

Second, it shows you are genuinely interested in working for the company since you had the forethought to prepare questions. Just imagine if the candidates you are up against brought no questions at all.

Believe me—a lot of candidates don't bring questions, and they miss out on a great opportunity to build rapport with the company.

There is not much else that you will need to prepare to bring for the interview. The most common items requested are your cover letter and resumé, transcripts, or a portfolio.

Now it's time to talk about your interview!

THE INTERVIEW!_

CONGRATULATIONS. You have received an interview invitation!

This is a big accomplishment. Your cover letter and resumé were strong enough to get a face-to-face meeting with the company. You have made great steps mastering the art of selling yourself. These are HUGE wins!

Now it's time to dive into everything interview!

———

I have sat at both sides of the interview table more times than I can count. I have been interviewed for well over 20 jobs, and interviewed hundreds of candidates. The information I'm about to share with you is not groundbreaking. There are some common themes in successful interviews and I'm sharing these themes below.

Rarely has a candidate's educational or work experience played the deciding factor in a hire. More often than not, the candidate's character, their honesty and integrity, their willingness to learn and grow are far more important factors than the degree they hold.

When hiring, I need to know the candidate will continue to focus on growth even when the times get tough. I look for a candidate who acknowledges there is always room for improvement, even if they have more than the requested experience.

Having a sense of humour can also be useful since it's easier to work through challenging times while having a laugh.

I understand interviews are tough and they can be uncomfortable. But they are necessary.

The company's objective is to find a candidate with valuable experience to turn into an employee.

The candidate's objective is to discover what the company considers valuable, and market those specific skills in the interview.

When these stars align, it makes the interview process straightforward for all parties involved.

Keep this in mind as you read the following information.

———

Strong interpersonal skills will help you land your dream job since communicating your value is step one. Interpersonal skills can be defined as the skills we use every day to communicate and interact with other people.

Therefore, do whatever you can to improve your interpersonal skills!

The three components of interpersonal skills are your body, voice, and mind.

Your body language can tell an interviewer whether you are friendly, tense, or relaxed. In the interview, try to come off as friendly and relaxed. A defensive posture, like crossing your arms, is not a welcoming look.

Your voice shows how confident you are in what you say. Remember that you are the expert on yourself and you know you the best. No one else can speak to your experience with as much authority as you can. Be confident when explaining your employment history.

Bring a confident mindset to the interview. Yes, this can be a challenging process, and the interviewer will ask you a lot of questions about your employment history. Remember that the company wants to see you successful. The interviewers are hoping you're the answer they've been looking for. Relish and enjoy the opportunity to bring what you know to the table.

With this being said, please know the interviewer will understand that you will be nervous. No one enjoys sitting in front of a panel of interviewers and being questioned about employment history.

Take a big breath, exhale nice and slow, and enjoy the process.

Below are three traits you should focus on to make the best first impression possible:

1. Friendly personality

2. Professional attitude

3. Organizational fit

At the end of the day, the company wants to know if you'd be a good fit with the rest of the team.

Are you friendly? Will you present this quality to the company and to customers?

Were you punctual and honest? Are you someone a company could invest in for the long term? Did you prepare more than other candidates? Did you ask good questions at the end of the interview?

Are you a good fit in terms of the company's values? Do you align with the organization's objectives and purpose? If you're applying to Google, did you prove that you're an outside-the box thinker? If you apply to work for the Red Cross, can you demonstrate empathy and a drive to help others?

These questions will help the hiring manager decide if you will be a good fit for the company.

You may have all the talent in the world, but if you're not professional, companies will not take the risk of hiring you.

So, how else can we prepare and show our professionalism? Arrive fifteen minutes early to your interview!

Punctuality is just as important as your degree, if not more. No one wants a NASA scientist at mission control who can't make the launch on time. If you start this employment relationship off by being late, you can pretty much say goodbye to a job offer.

Greet your interviewer with a firm handshake and a friendly smile. Introduce yourself, and relax. Remember, you're simply reiterating information you know and have prepared for.

At the end of the interview, shake hands with the interviewer once again and thank them for their time. Even if you think you bombed the interview, end the interaction on a happy note. Don't leave the interviewer with any kind of negative impression.

Leave them with good thoughts about you and your ability to bring results to their company.

In the next chapter, I'll discuss a few things to avoid doing in the interview that could cost you the job. Let's take a look.

WHAT NOT TO DO IN THE INTERVIEW_

NOW THAT YOU know how to make your interview a success, let's talk about a few things to avoid doing. You'll put forth effort to build trust with the company, but one misstep can cost you the job.

In the cover letter chapter, we talked about how important it is not to bring up topics like race, political affiliations, religious beliefs, or marital status. Leave these things out of the interview, too.

This is not to disqualify your character or beliefs. Nor am I intending to persuade you to leave who you are as a person out of the discussion.

The reason I make this suggestion is twofold.

First, your number one aim in an interview is to land a job. Only discuss the most relevant topics around employment history and value.

Second, we all know these topics can ignite passionate responses from people. It's best to focus on what value you'll bring to the company as a qualified professional. Once you have the job, you'll have all the time in the world to discuss what makes you, *you*.

Below, I've listed more things to keep in mind for your interview.

Maintain a professional demeanour. Be friendly, but not overly friendly during the interview. You may get along well with the interviewer but stay professional.

Swearing, blaming others, or complaining about previous employers are all red flags. Have fun with the interview and enjoy the time you have together, but never forget your objective.

Never lie about your work experience or the qualifications you hold. Integrity is a major component in the hiring process. It's hard to build trust back, and you may never have another opportunity. Lying about your qualifications or experience can blacklist you from online search engines.

Understand and admit to any weaknesses you have. Identifying personal weaknesses is a strength, especially if you can communicate how you have taken steps to improve in the area.

Do not bring your cell phone to the interview. Leave it in the car. It is extremely unprofessional for it to go off in the middle of your interview.

Do not, under any circumstance, blame others when speaking about past work experiences. You'll likely be asked about a time you had a difficult situation with a coworker. When you do, take extreme ownership over your professional career.

Hiring managers do not have respect for candidates who do not take accountability for their actions.

Discussing wage expectations can be very tricky, particularly if you have never negotiated before. Before your interview, check out Glassdoor on Google to research a wage range. If you're asked about wage expectations, provide a range you'd accept for the position instead of a single number. This way, the employer knows there's room on the table to negotiate, and you won't cut yourself short.

And there you have it. Now you know the common mistakes candidates make. Use this information to prepare for your next interview. Avoid problematic conversations that may inhibit landing your dream job.

In the next chapter, I'll debrief you with how you can use this book to take your job search to the next level. Let's take a look at what's coming next for you.

YOU DID IT!_

MY GOAL in writing this book is to help you land your dream job. I know these strategies work as I've used them to land *my* dream job.

Having supported hundreds of candidates to write effective cover letters and resumés, I've participated in almost as many interviews (at both sides of the hiring table!). I know what strategies work at every stage of the hiring process, plus the strategies that don't.

Every single thing I've learned since starting in the Career Resource nine years ago is now in this book.

Ninety-eight percent of candidates don't land their dream job because they do not communicate their value in their cover letter, resumé, or interview.

The reason the two percent of candidates succeed is because they understand the employer's needs, and they over-deliver in each step of the job search process.

I promise you, if you take action from this book, you will join the two percent and land the dream job you've been waiting for.

Urgent Plea!
Think You Could Leave A Review?

Thank you SO much for reading my book!

I really appreciate all of your feedback. It's great to hear what you have to say, and I need your input to make the next version of this book and my future books even better :)

I'd love to hear about any success you have landing your next job by leaving a review on Amazon.

Thank you :)

Michael Lachance